Marbury v. Madison

Powers of the Supreme Court

David DeVillers

Landmark Supreme Court Cases

This book is dedicated to my daughter,
Quinn Rachel DeVillers

Library of Congress Cataloging-in-Publication Data

DeVillers, David.
Marbury v. Madison: powers of the Supreme Court / David DeVillers.
p. cm. — (Landmark Supreme Court cases)
Includes bibliographical references and index.
Summary: Discusses the case Marbury v. Madison in which the idea of judicial review became part of the federal government's system of checks and balances.
ISBN 0-89490-967-3
1. Judicial review—United States—History—Juvenile literature.
2. Marbury, William, 1761 or 2–1835—Trials, litigation, etc.—
Juvenile literature. 3. Madison, James, 1751–1836—Trials,
litigation, etc.—Juvenile literature. [1. Judicial review.
2. Marbury, William, 1761 or 2–1835—Trials, litigation, etc.
3. Madison, James, 1751–1836—Trials, litigation, etc.] I. Title.
II. Series.
KF4575.Z9D48 1998
347.73' 12—dc21 97–24865
CIP
AC

Printed in the United States of America

10 9 8 7 6 5 4 3 2 1

Photo Credits: Reproduced from the Collections of the Library of Congress, pp. 8, 17, 23, 26, 31, 43, 47, 52, 57, 59, 65, 75, 81, 86, 90.

Cover Photo: Franz Jantzen, "Collection of the Supreme Court of the United States" (background); Reproduced form the Collections of the Library of Congress (inset).

Contents

1

A Young Constitution

Judicial review is the power that the United States Supreme Court has to review the actions of other branches of government and the states. It includes the power to review laws passed by Congress and to decide if those laws are in conflict with the United States Constitution. If they are, the Court may declare them unconstitutional—thus making them invalid. This power started early in our nation's history. It has since grown and expanded into one of the most powerful tools in all of government. It has been used to stop government from acting in areas where it does not have authority. It has also been used to protect the individual rights of the people. On occasion, the power of judicial review has, however, caused the government to operate more slowly.

Today the concept of judicial review is well established. The power of the Supreme Court comes from the Constitution itself. So it follows that the power of judicial review also must come from the Constitution. Yet, nowhere in the Constitution does it specifically state that the Supreme Court may reverse laws passed by Congress. How did this come to be?

Judges, lawyers, politicians, teachers, and students have all attempted to interpret the Constitution. Different people have different opinions as to what our Founding Fathers had in mind when they wrote the Constitution over two hundred years ago.

In 1803 the Constitution was only fourteen years old. The leaders of our country were the same people who wrote the Constitution. How easy it must have been for them to agree on what they meant only fourteen years earlier—right? Wrong. The leaders of our young country found themselves divided into two political parties. The first group was called the Federalists. Those who belonged believed in a strong central government that would be superior in power to the individual states. The second group was the Anti-Federalists. Those who belonged believed in a weak central government, with each state having superior power within its borders. The two sides were bitterly opposed to one another. Each side knew that the party that had the power, the final word on what the Constitution meant, would define our young country forever.

In 1803 the Anti-Federalists held power in two of the three branches of government. The executive branch was headed by the newly elected President Thomas Jefferson, an Anti-Federalist. The legislative branch, the lawmakers in Congress, was now dominated by Anti-Federalists. Only the judicial branch, the Supreme Court, was controlled by Federalists. The newly appointed Chief Justice of the Supreme Court was the Federalist John Marshall.

Just before Jefferson took office, the defeated Federalist President John Adams appointed a staunch Federalist by the name of William Marbury as a justice of the peace. Marbury's title, however, would not take effect until a commission, a formal, written document granting him the powers to perform his job, was delivered to him. By some oversight, the commission was not delivered before Adams left office. When Jefferson took office he, in effect, refused to honor Marbury's appointment. He told his secretary of state, James Madison, not to deliver the commission. Marbury went directly to the Supreme Court asking it to order Madison to deliver the commission.

At the time, the Supreme Court was seen as the

James Madison (shown here) was secretary of state under newly elected President Thomas Jefferson. Jefferson told Madison not to deliver the commission that would have allowed William Marbury and the rest of former President John Adams's appointees to become judges.

weakest of the three branches of government. Its power and authority were virtually untested. As Chief Justice of the Supreme Court, Marshall had to decide whether to grant Marbury's request and order Madison to deliver the commission. If he decided not to, Marshall would be abandoning a fellow Federalist. In addition, Marbury was entitled to make the request under existing law. If Marshall did grant the request and order Madison to deliver the commission, he recognized that Jefferson might just ignore the order. This would destroy any authority the Supreme Court had. Furthermore, such a decision would certainly anger the Anti-Federalist Congress. It could impeach, or bring to trial and attempt to remove from office, the Federalists on the Supreme Court—including Marshall.

In the end, Marshall's decision would set the stage for every Supreme Court case from that time forward. His decision would give the Supreme Court the final word on interpreting what the Constitution meant. This is where we must look at the origins of American judicial review. We must look beyond the Constitution itself into the events, politics, and personalities surrounding the case of *Marbury* v. *Madison.*

2

Personalities and Political Parties

The first President of the United States, George Washington, was not an official member of any political party. Every president after him was a member of some political party. The importance of these parties cannot be underestimated. They define a politician's political thought. They also organize and finance a campaign to elect this politician to office. Today the Republicans and Democrats dominate United States politics. Soon after the Constitutional Convention in Philadelphia in 1787, where the Constitution was drafted, our country's first two political parties emerged. They were the Federalists and the Anti-Federalists. The Anti-Federalists were also called

Republicans but had nothing to do with the Republican party as we know it today.

Once the United States won its independence from England it formed the Articles of Confederation. The Articles of Confederation created a very weak union between the thirteen existing states. Each state printed its own money and began to tax the goods being sold in its state by another state. Soon competition among the states began to threaten the existence of the young country. There was a need for a stronger central government with at least some power over the states. There was also, however, a fear that the states would lose too much power.

In 1786 a group of men met at Annapolis, Maryland, to try to solve these problems. Two of these men would have a huge impact on the future of our country. These two very different men were Alexander Hamilton and James Madison.

Alexander Hamilton was born in 1755 on the island of Nevis in the British West Indies. His mother and father were not married when he was born. In eighteenth century America, this created a large social barrier. He came to mainland America in 1772 and enrolled in King's College, now Columbia University, in New York City. He was young and had a great political mind. But he also had a temper that would make him many enemies. He became popular as he wrote articles attacking British treatment of the colonies. At the outbreak of the American Revolution (1775–1783), Hamilton became a military captain and formed an artillery company. Throughout the war he demonstrated a great intellect for the military. General George Washington noticed the young captain and made him one of his top advisers. After the war Hamilton practiced law in New York City.

James Madison was born into a wealthy Virginia family in 1751. He graduated from Princeton University in 1771. He too gained recognition for his anti-British writings. Because Madison was physically very small he could not serve in the Continental Army. As he continued to write anti-British propaganda he involved himself in Virginia politics. It was here that he met and became close friends with fellow Virginian Thomas Jefferson.

After the Revolution both Hamilton and Madison openly criticized the Articles of Confederation. They saw the Articles as ineffective. They wanted to centralize the government. They met at the Annapolis Convention and pushed for a convention to change or completely get rid of the Articles. They were in favor of a new constitution. They succeeded and a Constitutional Convention would gather in Philadelphia in May 1787.

Hamilton and Madison met again at the Constitutional Convention. They were delegates for their individual states. They contributed greatly to forming the new government and drafting the Constitution. In the end, not everything each man wanted in the Constitution was put in. They fought hard, however, to get the Constitution ratified, or accepted, by the states.

To convince the people of New York to ratify the Constitution, Madison and Hamilton once again joined forces. With the help of another New Yorker, John Jay, they wrote a collection of papers later published as a book called *The Federalist Papers.* These papers attempted to explain and offered interpretations of the Constitution. Even today, the *Federalist Papers* is considered one of the greatest works of political science ever written. These papers succeeded in convincing New York to ratify the Constitution. The other states also voted for ratification. In this way, the Constitution and the new government of the United States was formed.

The Constitution formed the three branches of the federal government. It also established the relationship between the federal government and the individual states. The Constitution did, however, leave room for interpretation. The debate over what the Constitution meant in regard to the relationship between the federal government and the states would result in the two political parties.

Hamilton and Madison would be among the leaders of these parties. But they would no longer be working together. They would become political enemies. However, they would not be the only partners turned enemies.

Thomas Jefferson and John Adams were among the political leaders of the Revolution. Like Madison, Jefferson was born into a wealthy Virginia family. He attended the College of William and Mary and eventually studied law. Although not a great speaker, he was renowned for his ability to write. He was elected a member of the body that led the Revolution, the Continental Congress. There he was placed on a committee to draft the Declaration of Independence. He was given the responsibility of actually writing the document. While in the Continental Congress, he met John Adams.

Adams was born in Massachusetts in 1735. He graduated from Harvard University and also studied law. Just prior to the Revolution, he wrote in protest of Britain's taxing of the colonies. He was a member of a radical group supporting independence. During the Revolution, he was a member of the Continental Congress. He was one of the first to propose independence. He was on the committee to draft the Declaration of Independence. During this time, he and Jefferson became good friends and had the utmost respect for each other.

Each of these men had a position in the new government. Madison was elected a member of Congress and wrote the first ten amendments to the Constitution, commonly known as the Bill of Rights. Hamilton was made President Washington's secretary of the treasury. Jefferson was the secretary of state. Adams, who negotiated the peace treaty with England, was elected vice-president.

It was during this period that the differences in their political thought emerged. Jefferson and Hamilton had bitter arguments over the power of the new federal government. Adams agreed with Hamilton's philosophy of a strong federal government superior to the states. Madison sided with Jefferson's belief in a limited federal government, with most of the power still belonging to the states.

The new Constitution seemed to support both views. Hamilton and Adams relied on Article VI of the Constitution, which states in part:

> This Constitution, and the Laws of the United States which shall be made in Pursuance thereof; and all Treaties made, or which shall be made, under the Authority of the United States, shall be the supreme

> Law of The land; and the Judges in every State shall be bound thereby, any Thing in the Constitution or Laws of any State to the Contrary notwithstanding.[1]

This clause of the Constitution, often called the Supremacy Clause, tells the states that they must abide by the Constitution and any laws passed by the United States Congress. Adams and Hamilton argued that any laws passed by states that contradicted federal law are unconstitutional and therefore invalid. This philosophy created the Federalist Party.

Jefferson and Madison relied on the Tenth Amendment to the Constitution. It states: "The powers not delegated to the United States by the Constitution, nor prohibited to it by the States, are reserved to the States respectively, or to the people."[2] This means that powers not specifically granted to the federal government by the Constitution can be taken and used by the states. For example, the Constitution does not specifically give the power to educate the people to the federal government. Therefore, the states can and do control school systems. Jefferson and Madison argued that the federal government does not have the power to pass laws that infringe on or interfere with powers that should belong solely to the states. This philosophy created the Anti-Federalist party.

At the end of Washington's second and final term as

One of the authors of *The Federalist Papers,* Alexander Hamilton was instrumental in getting the Constitution ratified. Hamilton believed that the United States should have a strong central government.

president, both parties were well established. Hamilton was the leader of the Federalist party. John Adams was a presidential candidate, although Hamilton supported another Federalist candidate. The Anti-Federalists had their leader, Thomas Jefferson, as a presidential candidate. Adams won the election, and in March 1797 he became the second president of the United States. Today, each candidate has a running mate who becomes vice-president should the candidate win the election. In 1798, however, the second place candidate became vice-president. Jefferson was the second-place finisher and became Adams's vice-president.

In 1776 Jefferson and Adams worked together to draft the Declaration of Independence. In 1797, they became president and vice-president. Unlike in 1776, however, they would rarely work together. They had many political differences and their arguments were bitter and public.

Jefferson's and Adams's political differences reached a turning point when the Federalist-dominated Congress passed the Alien and Sedition Acts. These laws penalized "any person, citizen as well as alien, for any 'false, scandalous and malicious' statements against the president, either house of Congress, or the government, made with intent to defame them. . . ."[3]

The Alien and Sedition Acts were enacted as a

means to curb the "dangers" of domestic opposition in time of war. They were in reality, however, a weapon against domestic political opposition in time of peace.[4] Prosecutions under these laws were brought against four leading Anti-Federalist newspapers. There were at least twenty-five arrests and fifteen formal charges of crimes resulting in ten convictions. In all cases the people prosecuted were Anti-Federalists.[5]

The Anti-Federalists argued that the laws violated the First Amendment. They also argued that the power to enact such laws lay outside the constitutional authority of Congress. The First Amendment states in part that "Congress shall make no law . . . abridging the freedom of speech, or of the press." The Alien and Sedition Acts made it a crime for the people to make false, scandalous, and malicious statements against the president, John Adams, or the Congress. Most of the people being prosecuted were newspaper editors. Were these laws unconstitutional? If so, could anyone declare them invalid?

This was the first time a federal law's constitutionality was seriously challenged. The Constitution was not clear on how or where to make such a challenge. The Anti-Federalists did challenge the laws through lower federal courts. These courts, however, were packed with Federalists who upheld the law as constitutional. The Supreme Court itself never directly ruled on the constitutionality of the laws.

Both Jefferson, who was vice-president at the time, and Madison hated the Alien and Sedition Acts. They knew, however, that they could not defeat them through the courts. So they challenged the laws through the states. Near the end of 1798, they anonymously wrote the Kentucky and Virginia Resolutions. These Resolutions declared the Alien and Sedition Acts unconstitutional and inoperative in Kentucky and Virginia. They argued that the federal government was expanding its authority beyond its constitutional limits. This argument was consistent with the Anti-Federalist philosophy. According to this school of thought, the federal government should not interfere with the powers of the states.

The Kentucky and Virginia Resolutions were not warmly received by the rest of the country. Every other state rejected the idea that a state could declare an act of Congress unconstitutional.

Jefferson and Madison failed in their attempt to declare a federal law unconstitutional. The final word on what the Constitution meant did not belong to the states. Therefore, if it belonged to anyone, it must belong to the federal government. But which branch of the government?

3

Marbury's Commission

The Alien and Sedition Acts survived the Kentucky and Virginia Resolutions. They would not, however, survive the will of the people. The laws backfired on the Federalists. The people sympathized with the Anti-Federalists, and their popularity grew with every prosecution. In 1801 the Federalists would lose control of both Congress and the presidency.

The presidential election of 1800 was so close that two of the candidates, Thomas Jefferson and Aaron Burr, had the same number of electoral votes. Both candidates were Anti-Federalists, and both had more votes than John Adams. Thus Adams, the current president, was out of the race. According to the Constitution, a tie in the electoral vote requires Congress to decide which candidate will be president. This is the only time in

United States history that a presidential vote went to Congress.

While Congress was debating over the election, Adams, still president, wanted to pack the courts with as many Federalists as possible before the Anti-Federalists took office. The president has the power to appoint federal judges, including Supreme Court Justices. These judgeships have life terms. Federal judges cannot be fired by anyone. They can only be impeached by Congress. Impeachment, however, is very rare and extremely difficult to accomplish. So for the most part, once a federal judge is appointed it is his or her job until retirement. By appointing Federalists to judgeships, Adams could keep the Federalist philosophy alive for decades through the judiciary.

Adams needed to fill the recently vacated position of Chief Justice of the Supreme Court. He chose his secretary of state, the loyal Federalist John Marshall. Marshall would continue serving as the secretary of state until the new president took office. On February 4, 1801, Marshall was sworn in as the fourth Chief Justice of the Supreme Court.

Marshall was born on the Virginia frontier in 1755. He was not from a wealthy family and was largely self-educated. The only formal legal education he had came from six weeks of lectures at the College of William and

When John Adams (shown here) was not re-elected as president it meant that two Anti-Federalists, Thomas Jefferson and Aaron Burr, would be president and vice president. Therefore, Adams tried to appoint as many Federalists as possible as federal judges. This way, the Federalists would still control the judicial branch of the government.

Mary. During the Revolution, he served under George Washington. He was at Valley Forge and was considered a hero at the battles of Germantown and Brandywine. Back in Virginia, he competed with Thomas Jefferson for the affection of Rebecca Burwell.[1] Marshall married Burwell and started a long rivalry with Jefferson.

In 1788, he was a member of the Virginia State Constitutional Convention. He argued vigorously for ratification. He talked a great deal about the judiciary article of the proposed Constitution. Here, for the first time, he gave a hint on who he thought had the final word on the meaning of the Constitution. He said:

> [T]o make a law not warranted by any of the powers enumerated, it would be considered by judges as an infringement of the Constitution which they were to guard. . . . They would declare it void.[2]

This meant that the courts had a duty to guard against any laws passed by Congress that the Constitution does not give Congress power to rule over.

Marshall soon became the leader of the Federalist Party in Virginia and the enemy of Jefferson. Jefferson, giving his personal opinion of his fellow Virginian, called Marshall "hypocritical and cunning."[3] In 1797 Marshall represented his country in negotiations with France. They were trying to resolve rising tensions between the two countries. In 1798 he was elected to

Congress, and two years later President Adams made him secretary of state.

Alexander Hamilton disliked Jefferson but he hated Aaron Burr. Hamilton convinced the Federalists in Congress to choose the lesser of two evils when they voted to break the tie for the presidency. With the support of reluctant Federalists, Jefferson defeated Burr. He was elected president on February 17, 1801. He was to be sworn in on March 4 of the same year.

Congress, which was dominated by Federalists, did no better than the president in the elections of 1800. The Anti-Federalists were about to take control of Congress. On February 27, 1801, Congress gave Adams the opportunity to appoint even more Federalists to the judiciary. The Judiciary Act of 1801 gave the president the power to appoint as many justices of the peace as he thought were necessary.

The President-elect Thomas Jefferson was well aware of what his one-time friend Adams and the Federalists were up to. He wrote to a friend: "The Federalists have retired into the Judiciary as a stronghold . . . and from that battery all the works of republicanism [the Anti-Federalists] are to be beaten down and erased."[4] In the last sixteen days of his administration Adams appointed fifty-eight justices of the peace.

John Marshall (shown here) was appointed as Chief Justice of the Supreme Court while John Adams was president. Marshall was the leader of the Federalist Party in Virginia.

On March 3, 1801, the Senate confirmed forty-two justices of the peace. These commissions were signed and sealed by Adams before he left office. Once these commissions were delivered, the forty-two men would officially have their jobs as justices of the peace. But the commissions, through some oversight, were not delivered. They remained in the secretary of state's office when Jefferson took over on March 4th.

Jefferson's secretary of state was his longtime friend James Madison. When Madison took over as secretary of state he found himself in possession of the undelivered commissions. Jefferson ordered Madison not to deliver them. Furthermore, Jefferson viewed the commissions as invalid unless delivered. Eventually Jefferson allowed Madison to deliver twenty-five of the forty-two commissions. This left seventeen of the Adams's appointees unable to take office. One of these appointees was William Marbury.

Little is known about William Marbury. His fame comes from his filing a petition in the most important case in Supreme Court history. We do know that he was a wealthy Georgetown landowner. He was also an active and loyal member of the Federalist Party. His activity in the party was probably the reason Jefferson decided not to deliver the commission.

On December 16, 1801, Marbury and three other

Adams appointees filed a petition. The petition asked the Supreme Court to order Madison to deliver the commissions. John Marshall, who had been Chief Justice for only nine months, ordered a hearing on the matter at the Court's next session. This turned out to be over a year later, on February 10, 1803.

4

The Supreme Court

In order to understand the importance of the decision to come, it is necessary to know what the Supreme Court is and what it was like in 1803. Article III of the United States Constitution provides for "one Supreme Court, and in such inferior Courts as the Congress may from time to time ordain and establish."[1] The Constitution created the federal courts and defined the kinds of cases they would have authority over. The exact structure of the federal courts, however, was left up to Congress to create.

The Judiciary Act of 1789 provided for the structure of the federal courts. The structure resembled a pyramid with the Supreme Court at the top. Below the Supreme Court would be three circuit courts. These were the eastern, middle, and southern circuits. Below the circuit courts would be thirteen district courts. There would be one for each of the then-existing states. The district courts would be the trial courts. The circuit courts would hear any appeals from trials at the district court level. The Supreme Court would hear appeals from the circuit courts. The Supreme Court would have the final word.

The Judiciary Act also provided for six members of the Supreme Court, including a Chief Justice. Today there are a total of nine Supreme Court Justices. The Constitution gave the president the power to appoint the Justices. George Washington appointed John Jay as his first Chief Justice. Jay knew the Constitution well. He had served in the Continental Congress and co-authored the *Federalist Papers* in support of the new Constitution. Jay negotiated the Treaty of Paris in 1783, which ended the Revolutionary War. He also negotiated a second treaty with Britain in 1794, known as the Jay Treaty.

An early Supreme Court Justice could expect physically exhausting and sometimes dangerous work. When not in session with the Supreme Court, each Justice was required to sit on one of the three circuit courts. This involved lots of travel, and travel in the late eighteenth century was hazardous. The Justices would travel by horseback or carriages for days. They were robbed, were

The Supreme Court Building in Washington, D.C., is shown here.

victims of carriage accidents and violent weather, and had to combat disease, which spread quickly in the late eighteenth century. Because of these conditions, some of the best lawyers and state judges in the country would not accept appointments to the Supreme Court.

The term of a Supreme Court Justice is for life. This is to ensure the independence of the Court. With life terms, there is less pressure on the Court by political parties, special interest groups, and the other branches of government. The Justices can make decisions based on the law with no fear of losing their job.

Most Supreme Court cases come from its appellate jurisdiction. In other words, most cases are appeals from lower federal courts or state supreme courts on constitutional issues. Some cases come to the Supreme Court by *certiorari. Certiorari* occurs when one party contends that a lower court made a serious legal error and petitions the Supreme Court to review the case. Thousands of these petitions are made every year, but the Supreme Court grants *certiorari* in only a few.

When we think of courts we usually think of witnesses testifying and attorneys asking them questions in front of a jury. This is not how a Supreme Court hearing is conducted. The attorneys for each side first submit written arguments called briefs. These briefs state the position of each side and why the Court should rule in its favor. They may cite an existing law, sections of the Constitution, or even an earlier Supreme Court decision that favors their side's point of view. After the Supreme Court Justices have read these briefs, they hear arguments of counsel (attorneys). Here the Justices have the opportunity to ask the attorneys more specific questions.

Once all of the arguments are heard, the Justices discuss the case in private among themselves. They then vote on the decision. Not all of the decisions are unanimous. The majority opinion among the Justices wins. If the Chief Justice is in the majority, he or she may write the decision. Otherwise, the senior Justice in the majority decides which Justice will write the majority opinion. The written decision is called the opinion. Justices who agree with the decision but not the reasons behind it may write what is called a concurring opinion. Justices in the minority, those who disagree with the decision, may write a dissenting opinion.

In the early years the Supreme Court was seen as the weakest by far of the three branches of government. Its unimportance in national politics can be shown by the small number of opinions it rendered in the first ten years of its existence. From 1790 to 1800, it wrote fewer than seventy opinions.[2]

The Constitution set up an entire system of

government where checks and balances would ensure that one branch of government would not dominate the others. Yet the Supreme Court never even came close to challenging the power of the legislative (Congress) or executive (President) branches of government. This would all change in 1803. John Marshall's decision would thrust the Supreme Court into the center of the nation's politics.

5

The Decision

On February 10, 1803, the case of *Marbury* v. *Madison* was heard before the Supreme Court. Each side had an opportunity to argue its case in front of Chief Justice Marshall and the rest of the Supreme Court. The attorney representing Marbury was Charles Lee. He was the former attorney general under the Adams administration. The attorney representing Madison was Jefferson's attorney general, Levi Lincoln. He had submitted only a written argument.

The Argument

Lee argued that the appointment of Marbury was valid and that he had a right to receive the commission. Furthermore, the Supreme Court had the power and jurisdiction to order Madison to deliver the commission under the Judiciary Act of 1789. Through this act, Congress authorized the Supreme Court "to issue writs of mandamus in cases warranted by the principles and usages of law, to any courts appointed, or persons holding office, under the authority of the United States."[1]

A writ is simply a court order. A writ of *mandamus* is a special court order that forces a government official to perform a mandatory duty that he or she has failed to perform. Lee argued that Madison was, as secretary of state, a "person holding office under the authority of the United States."[2] Madison was, therefore, obligated to perform duties prescribed by law, including delivering Marbury's commission.

Lincoln argued only that the issue was purely political, not legal. As such, the Supreme Court should ignore Marbury's request and not order Madison to deliver the commission.

The Opinion

It took the Court two weeks to come to its decision. Marshall was in a seemingly no-win situation. If he ruled in favor of Marbury and granted the writ, Jefferson would surely ignore the order. The effect of this on the Court's already almost-powerless status would be devastating. On the other hand, if Marshall denied the writ, the Court would be seen as backing down. The effect would be the same. On February 24, 1803, Marshall issued the Court's opinion.

Is this a political issue?

Marshall began by addressing Levi Lincoln's argument that this was a purely political issue. He recognized that the "province of the court is, solely, to decide on the rights of individuals, not to inquire how the executive, or executive officers, perform duties in which they have a discretion."[3] This holds true today. The Supreme Court has always avoided political questions. As long as political officeholders are acting within their powers and not violating others' rights, the Court will not interfere.

So, Marshall had to decide if Marbury had a legal right to receive the commission. If not, then it would be a purely political question and the Court would not have jurisdiction to go further. If so, then the decision would be about the rights of an individual and *would* fall under the Court's jurisdiction. The office that Marbury was appointed to was for a term of five years, and was irrevocable. That is, the president could not fire him, and he would remain a justice of the peace for at least five years. Marbury would not be a mere employee that the president could fire at will. If the commission was delivered, the president could not replace Marbury for at least five years.

Marshall found that this was a legal, not a political matter. Since the president signed the commission and the secretary of state sealed it, Marbury had a legal right to the commission. Ironically, Marshall himself was the secretary of state who sealed but failed to deliver the commission.

Does the Supreme Court have the legal authority to order the secretary of state to deliver the commission?

It had been decided that this was not a political question, and that Marbury had a legal right to the commission. The next step was to decide whether the Supreme Court had the power and authority to order Madison to deliver the commission.

The Judiciary Act of 1789 allowed the Court to order public servants to carry out their legal obligations. James Madison, as Secretary of State, was a public servant. Since Marbury had a legal right to the commission, Madison had a legal duty to deliver it. So at least according to the Judiciary Act of 1789, Marbury should be granted his writ.

Is the Judiciary Act of 1789 in conflict with the Constitution?

The Judiciary Act of 1789 clearly authorized the Supreme Court to issue a writ of *mandamus*. This act of

Congress set up the structure of the Supreme Court as well as all of the federal courts. The Supreme Court derives its power from the Constitution, however, not the Judiciary Act of 1789. Marshall looked at the act and the Constitution and found a conflict between the two. Article III, section 2, of the Constitution states:

> In all cases affecting Ambassadors, other public Ministers and Consuls, and those in which a State shall be a Party, the supreme Court shall have original Jurisdiction. In all the other Cases before mentioned, the supreme Court shall have appellate jurisdiction. . . .[4]

Original jurisdiction refers to the starting place of the case. The district courts are usually where cases start. They have original jurisdiction. A person who loses in a district court can appeal to a circuit court. The Supreme Court has jurisdiction over both the district and circuit courts. It is the top of the pyramid. After the Supreme Court, there is nowhere else to appeal.

The Constitution grants the Supreme Court original jurisdiction in only two situations. The first is in cases involving ambassadors, public ministers, and counsels. This basically covers individuals representing foreign countries. The second is in cases where two states are involved. For example, if New York were suing Pennsylvania over money owed to it on a road built between the two states, the Supreme Court could hear that case directly. It would not be necessary for a lower court to hear the case first. The Constitution specifically limits the Supreme Court's original jurisdiction to these and only these types of cases.

The Judiciary Act of 1789 allows a party to go directly to the Supreme Court and request a writ of *mandamus.* This attempted to grant original jurisdiction to the Supreme Court—something the Constitution did not permit. Marshall wrote: "The authority . . . given to the Supreme Court, by the Act establishing the judicial courts of the United States, to issue writs of mandamus to public officers, appears not to be warranted by the Constitution."[5] This meant that the Judiciary Act of 1789 gave power to the Supreme Court that the Constitution did not allow.

What if Congress granted the district or circuit courts the power to issue a writ of *mandamus*? This would not be in conflict with the Constitution. The Constitution is silent as to what these lower courts have original jurisdiction over. In fact, the Supreme Court could hear appeals from these lower courts on a writ of *mandamus.* Article III, section 2, of the Constitution grants the Supreme Court appellate jurisdiction in "all the other Cases."

What should be done about a law in conflict with the Constitution?

What Marshall wrote next is what makes *Marbury* v. *Madison* the most important case in Supreme Court history. This is the landmark that establishes judicial review. The section of the Judiciary Act of 1789 granting the Supreme Court the power to issue writs of *mandamus* was in conflict with the Constitution. Marshall's next task was to decide which to follow, the United States Constitution or the Judiciary Act of 1789. The answer to this question would have long-term effects. When an act (a law passed by Congress) *and* the Constitution apply to a given case, which is to be followed?

The Constitution established the United States government. It defined the government's powers. Just as importantly, the Constitution defined the limits of that power. The Constitution contains the rules under which our government works. Marshall felt that the Constitution must, therefore, be superior to an act of Congress. After all, Congress must act within the rules set out by the Constitution. He wrote, "Certainly all those who have framed written constitutions contemplate them as forming the fundamental and paramount law of the nation. . . ."[6] When an act of Congress and the Constitution are in conflict, the Constitution must be followed.

What became of the Judiciary Act of 1789?

The Judiciary Act of 1789, at least the section applying to writs of *mandamus,* became void. Since this section of the act had to yield to the supremacy of the Constitution, it lost its effect. Marshall proclaimed that any "act repugnant to the constitution, is void."[7]

How could the Supreme Court strike down an act of Congress?

Remember that at the time of this decision the Supreme Court was seen as the weakest branch of the government. The legislature was seen as the strongest branch. As such, it was necessary for Marshall to show how the Supreme Court got the power to void an act of Congress.

> It is emphatically the province and duty of the judiciary department to say what the law is. Those who apply the rule to particular cases, must of necessity expound and interpret that rule. If two laws conflict with each other, the courts must decide on the operation of each.[8]

The Constitution does not specifically grant any branch of government the power of judicial review. But Marshall argued that it would be useless to create a Supreme Court if the Constitution did not allow it to be the final word on the law. If the Supreme Court is not the final word on what the law is, it ultimately has no power and it would have been meaningless to create it in the first place.

The Constitution formed the rules for the government. It is up to the Supreme Court to make sure the government follows those rules. Marshall asked, "Why does a judge swear to discharge his duties agreeable to the Constitution of the United States, if that constitution forms no rule for his government?"[9]

Did Marbury get his writ of *mandamus*?

Marbury's request for a court order to force Madison to deliver his commission was denied. Marshall clearly stated that Marbury was entitled to the commission

A view of what the Capitol building looked like in 1850 is shown here. Both the House of Representatives and the Senate hold session here.

under the law. But the law giving the Supreme Court the power to grant such an order was unconstitutional.

The Supreme Court is the final word on what the Constitution means

A law in conflict with the Constitution is void. The Supreme Court is the final word in deciding which laws are in conflict with the Constitution. Therefore, the Supreme Court has the power to declare a law passed by Congress void.

Marbury's loss was the Supreme Court's gain. In one decision, the Supreme Court declared itself the master of the Constitution. The power, the final word on what the Constitution means, belonged not to the president, not to Congress, but to the Supreme Court.

In 1789 Jefferson and Madison wrote the Virginia and Kentucky Resolutions. This was an attempt to invalidate an act of Congress (the Alien and Sedition Acts). They did not succeed. Now Marshall wrote a Supreme Court decision invalidating an act of Congress. Would the rest of the country allow the Supreme Court to do what they did not allow the Virginia and Kentucky Resolutions to do? Would the President, Congress, and the people accept the decision in *Marbury* v. *Madison*? Would the country accept the concept of judicial review?

6

The Supreme Court Survives *Marbury v. Madison*

President Jefferson was outraged by the Supreme Court's decision. Jefferson won because Madison was not ordered to deliver the commission. But he lost because the Federalist-controlled Supreme Court now claimed the power to invalidate acts of Congress. Jefferson never officially recognized the power of judicial review. He believed that each branch of government had separate and equal powers. As such, each branch could decide the validity of an act of Congress on its own. It could act independently according to its opinion on a particular act.

Jefferson and the Anti-Federalists feared that the

Supreme Court would now find all acts passed by the newly elected Anti-Federalist Congress invalid. Acting on this fear, Jefferson set out on a campaign to intimidate or eliminate the Federalists on the Court. Even before the Court's decision in *Marbury* v. *Madison,* Anti-Federalists moved to impeach Federalist judges. A leading Anti-Federalist congressman, William Branch Gills, wrote to Jefferson just after his 1801 inauguration, "It appears to me that the only check upon the judiciary system as it is now organized and filled is the removal of all its [judges] indiscriminately."[1]

Impeachment of a federal judge can be accomplished only through a trial in the United States Senate. In 1804, the Anti-Federalists were successful in impeaching a Federalist district court judge from New Hampshire named John Pickering. They now set their sights on the Supreme Court itself.

Supreme Court Justice Samuel Chase, who concurred (agreed) with Marshall's opinion in *Marbury* v. *Madison,* was hated by the Anti-Federalists. Chase was a strong supporter of the Alien and Sedition Acts, which targeted Anti-Federalist newspapers for prosecution. Chase did not care much for the Anti-Federalists. In a remark to a Baltimore grand jury he demonstrated this dislike by criticizing the Anti-Federalists. The speech was considered inappropriate for a judge.

Thomas Jefferson was frustrated with the outlook of the Federalist members of the Supreme Court and even attempted to remove one of them from the Court.

Impeachment proceedings against Chase began. At his trial, lawyers for Chase argued that Jefferson was attempting to destroy the independence of the judiciary by attacking Chase. The senate agreed and Chase was acquitted (not impeached) by a narrow margin.

Jefferson had failed to impeach a Supreme Court Justice. He had, however, showed a willingness to try. Jefferson also had seen that he did not have the support of Congress. He could not impeach the Supreme Court Justices "indiscriminately." In any event, Jefferson's fear that the Supreme Court would randomly invalidate acts of Congress did not become a reality. In fact, it would be over fifty years until it would next invalidate an act of Congress. This restraint by Marshall and the rest of the Supreme Court, along with the failure to impeach Chase, ended further efforts to impeach the Supreme Court Justices.

Unlike the Virginia and Kentucky Resolutions, the concept of judicial review was accepted by the people. The other two branches of government, although somewhat reluctantly, eventually accepted judicial review. The philosophies of Federalism and Anti-Federalism would clash until Anti-Federalism's violent conclusion at the end of the Civil War. Marshall would continue to enlarge the philosophies of judicial review and Federalism by applying them to the states.

7

Out of Thin Air

Did Marshall invent judicial review? Did he just pluck the concept out of thin air? In the Supreme Court's opinion in *Marbury* v. *Madison,* to justify judicial review, Marshall relied completely on deductive reasoning. The Constitution does not specifically state that the Supreme Court has the power of judicial review. But Marshall reasoned that the power exists from what the Constitution *does* specifically state. He cited no authority to support this interpretation of the Constitution. But such authority did exist. Many of Marshall's contemporaries shared his belief that the Constitution granted the power of judicial review. Jefferson, of course, was not one of them.

The United States adopted its legal system from England. The United States was an English colony, and the lawyers of the time were trained in the English legal tradition. Judicial review in one form or another had existed in England for a century prior to Marshall's decision. Many felt that it only made sense that judicial review would be adopted along with the rest of English legal procedures.

During the Constitutional Convention there was debate as to whether Article III, which created the judiciary, carried with it the authority to allow the judiciary to rule over acts of Congress and state laws. James Madison took extensive notes on the convention. These notes are the only real record of what was argued at the convention. His notes indicated that no fewer than twenty-six delegates spoke about the need for judicial review.[1] In the final draft of the Constitution, however, the power of judicial review was never expressly stated. This could be because the delegates, like Marshall, believed that the power was implied.

Probably the most convincing authority on the legitimacy of judicial review are the "Federalist Papers." These papers were written in a series of newspaper articles. They were meant to convince the people of the state of New York to ratify the Constitution. The "Federalist Papers" started to appear in the New York press beginning on October 27, 1787. They were written by John Jay, James Madison, and Alexander Hamilton. These men would later become political rivals. At the time, however, they joined together for the common goal of ratifying the Constitution.

Federalist article number seventy-eight was written by Hamilton. In that article, he explained the judiciary. He explained how it worked, the power it would have, and why it was necessary. He wrote:

> A Constitution is, in fact, and must be regarded by the judges, as fundamental law. It therefore belongs to them to ascertain its meaning, as well as the meaning of any particular act proceeding from the legislative body.[2]

It seems clear from this statement that the drafters of the Constitution *did* intend the Supreme Court to be the interpreter of the Constitution. Hamilton goes on to explain that when the legislature (Congress) passes a law in conflict with the Constitution "the Constitution ought to be preferred to the statute [law]."[3]

After the *Marbury* decision Thomas Jefferson and the Anti-Federalists argued strongly against the Supreme Court having the power of judicial review. But only a few years earlier many Anti-Federalists had been asking the courts to declare the Alien and Sedition Acts unconstitutional. It appeared that many Anti-Federalists recognized the power of judicial review, at least when it favored their cause. After the *Marbury* decision, however, they denied the existence of the same power they had attempted to use a few years earlier.

In his Supreme Court opinion of *Marbury* v. *Madison,* Chief Justice John Marshall is credited with establishing the idea of judicial review within the federal government.

The people who wrote the Constitution were the same people who were in power at the time of *Marbury* v. *Madison.* This could explain why Marshall never cited English common law, the debates at the Constitutional Convention, or the "Federalist Papers." Perhaps he felt the power was so clear that he only needed to cite the Constitution itself. Marshall did not invent judicial review. The concept was there waiting for the opportunity to be used. Few thought it would be used in *Marbury* v. *Madison,* but Marshall had the opportunity, and he took it.

8

Federal Supremacy and State Judicial Review

It is important to remember that Marshall was a Federalist. He believed in a strong federal government where federal laws were superior to state laws. Like Adams and Hamilton he felt that the Supremacy Clause of the Constitution made federal law the final word.

By 1819 most of the uproar over the Supreme Court's decision in *Marbury* v. *Madison* had subsided. Judicial review of federal laws seemed to be accepted by the other two branches of government. What about judicial review of state laws? Could the Supreme Court invalidate a law passed by state lawmakers?

As early as 1796, the Supreme Court had invalidated state laws that interfered with United States treaties with Great Britain. It was widely accepted that the federal government had exclusive power over international affairs. These cases drew little attention or criticism. Now Marshall and the Supreme Court would attempt to strike down a state law that dealt with a purely state-related issue.

McCulloch v. *Maryland:* The Arguments

In the early 1800s, the national bank was the hot political topic. The national bank was a bank established and run by the federal government. It had numerous branches throughout the country. The Federalists were strong supporters of the bank. It was a safe place for people to put their money, and it was a source of money from which the country could invest. The Anti-Federalists saw the bank as an expansion of federal power, which they intensely opposed.

On February 11, 1818, the Maryland General Assembly (Maryland's lawmakers) enacted a law imposing a tax on branches of the national bank that did business in Maryland. A very heavy tax was imposed on the Baltimore branch of the national bank. The bank's cashier, James McCulloch, challenged the tax as unconstitutional. That same year, the Supreme Court heard arguments by both sides in the case that would be known as *McCulloch* v. *Maryland.*

McCulloch argued that the bank was a federal operation established by federal law. Federal law is superior to state law. Therefore, any state law interfering with federal law must be invalid. Since Maryland's law taxing the national bank interfered with a federal law, it must be invalid.

The state of Maryland argued that the federal law establishing the national bank was unconstitutional. The federal government did not have the constitutional authority to run such an operation. Maryland also argued that the law was merely a tax on a business operating in the state, which could be taxed like any other business.

McCulloch v. *Maryland:* The Opinions

The arguments were clearly divided down party lines. The Federalists sided with McCulloch and the Anti-Federalists with the state of Maryland. Marshall was still the Chief Justice of the Supreme Court, and the Court was still dominated by Federalists. Would Marshall use judicial review to strike down a state law as he did with a federal law in *Marbury* v. *Madison*?

Does the federal government have the power to establish a national bank?

Marshall recognized that the Constitution does not specifically state that the federal government has the power to create a national bank. The Constitution does, however, grant specific powers to Congress. These are called enumerated powers. These powers include the power "to lay and collect Taxes, . . . To borrow Money, . . . To regulate Commerce, . . . To declare War, . . . [and] To raise and support Armies and . . . a Navy."[1]

The Constitution allows Congress to make any laws that are "necessary and proper" to execute the enumerated powers.[2] This is called the Necessary and Proper Clause. For example, Congress has the enumerated power to raise and support an army. Since a draft of civilians may be necessary and proper to raise an army, it is allowed by the Constitution. Congress also has the enumerated power to borrow money. A national bank allows Congress to borrow money from the people depositing it in the bank. Therefore, a national bank is necessary and proper to meet the enumerated power of borrowing money.

Can a state tax the federal government?

Marshall next addressed Maryland's argument that the law was merely a tax on a business operating in the state. During the Constitutional Convention of 1787 Marshall strongly denounced the Articles of Confederation. These articles allowed states to tax the

We the People of the United States, in order to form a more perfect Union, establish Justice,

Article. I

There have been numerous debates about exactly which powers the federal government is given in the Constitution. All powers not given to the federal government are given to the states and the people. The national bank was one topic that caused arguments between people who believed in a strong federal government, and those who pushed for states' rights.

goods and services of other states. Seeing that a tax can be a powerful weapon, Marshall wrote:

> The power to tax involves the power to destroy . . . this is a tax on the operations of the bank, and is, consequently, a tax on the operation of an instrument employed by the government of the union to carry its powers into execution. Such a law must be unconstitutional.[3]

Marshall would not allow the states to interfere with the business of the federal government. To allow a state to tax the federal government would greatly interfere with its power to operate.

The Federal Government is Supreme

In his opinion Marshall briefly mentioned the Tenth Amendment. "The powers not delegated to the United States by the Constitution, nor prohibited by it to the States, are reserved to the States respectively or the people." This is the section of the Constitution on which the Anti-Federalists rely most. It seems to support Maryland's argument to be able to tax the bank. But Marshall countered. He cited the section of the Constitution on which the Federalists rely most, the Supremacy Clause. He wrote: "The government of the United States though limited in its powers, is supreme; and its laws, when in pursuance of the Constitution, form the supreme law of the land."[4]

Andrew Jackson shared Thomas Jefferson's belief in limiting the powers of the central government. In 1832, Jackson vetoed a bill that would have renewed the charter of the national bank. By 1836 the national bank was no more.

Although this was not the first time Marshall had declared a state law unconstitutional, it was the most powerful example of the federal government's dominance over the states.[5] In invalidating Maryland's tax against the federal government, Marshall again expanded the power of judicial review over the states. At the same time, he again declared the federal government supreme.

9

The Legacy of Marbury v. Madison

The leaders of our nation's first political parties were the same men who helped to win our independence from Great Britain and to draft our Constitution. These men risked their fortune, freedom, and lives to form our nation. The political feuding that took place after ratification of the Constitution should not diminish their accomplishments.

James Madison became president after his friend Thomas Jefferson's second term ended. For his work on the Constitution and Bill of Rights, Madison is called the Father of the Constitution. Alexander Hamilton died as a result of his pride and stubbornness. Hamilton verbally attacked Aaron Burr's character. Hamilton did not want to see Burr become president and supported Jefferson instead. An angry Burr challenged Hamilton to a duel. Hamilton accepted and died of a gunshot wound in 1804. His work on the "Federalist Papers" and as the first secretary of the treasury, however, would secure his place in history as America's first great conservative mind.

John Adams lived to see his son, John Quincy Adams, become the sixth president of the United States. Thomas Jefferson went back to Virginia and established the University of Virginia. After their political careers Adams and Jefferson renewed their friendship. On July 4, 1776, both men risked everything they had in signing the Declaration of Independence. They worked together as friends in drafting the document. On July 4, 1826, the fiftieth anniversary of the signing of the Declaration of Independence, both men died, on the very same day, as friends.

John Marshall served as Chief Justice longer than any other person to date. He is known as the "Great Chief Justice" and the "Expounder of the Constitution." He is a perfect example of the right person in the right place at the right time. Without him, judicial review might not exist today. Without it, the Supreme Court could have been an insignificant branch of government. Marshall died in 1835. His opinions are still quoted by today's Supreme Court Justices.

William Marbury never became a judge. He eventually became a bank president, and apparently died a wealthy man. His name will forever be linked with the power of judicial review.

Today, in the Supreme Court building, there are portraits of two men side by side, as if they are about to start a prize fight. Those men are William Marbury and James Madison. The portraits illustrate the importance of *Marbury* v. *Madison* even today. The concepts behind the case and judicial review have grown and expanded into a tool for keeping in check the abuses of government. But as we will see, the tool also been misused.

Judicial Review After Marshall

The *Marbury* decision marked the first time a federal law was declared invalid by the Supreme Court. It was the only time John Marshall used judicial review to strike down a federal law. But the power was there, and Congress knew it. All federal laws from that time forward were written and passed with the knowledge that the Supreme Court could eventually review such laws. It was, therefore, important that Congress draft all laws so that they were consistent with the Constitution.

John Marshall's successor as Chief Justice was Roger B. Taney. He and his Court also showed a great deal of restraint in using the power of judicial review. In 1857, however, the Taney Court would strike down a federal law. In so doing, it would divide the country and help plunge the United States into the most devastating war in its history—the Civil War.

Dred Scott was the slave of a army surgeon named John Emerson. In 1834, Emerson took Scott from Missouri to army posts in the free state of Illinois and northern territory that would later become Minnesota. He stayed there until 1838. Congress had, some time before this, passed a law that became known as the Missouri Compromise. This law prohibited slavery in the part of the country into which Emerson took Scott. Relying on the Missouri Compromise, Scott brought suit in court seeking his freedom. After several trials and legal maneuvering in state and federal courts, the case found its way to the United States Supreme Court.

The case was *Scott* v. *Sandford* (the official Court spelling) in 1857. Chief Justice Taney wrote the opinion of the Court. The Court found that Congress lacked the power to prohibit slavery in the states or territories. The Missouri Compromise violated the Fifth Amendment's Due Process Clause. This clause states that Congress cannot deprive a citizen of "life, liberty or property, without due process of law." Since a slave, by definition, was property, Congress could not deny a citizen the right to own a slave.

The interior of the Supreme Court building is shown here. In 1857 the power of the Supreme Court to review both federal and state laws was reaffirmed in the *Dred Scott* case.

The issue of slavery and the conflicts between the states and the federal government divided the country into North and South. In 1861 the same political arguments that created the Federalist and Anti-Federalist parties some seventy years earlier were still unresolved. The North, like the Federalists, believed in a strong federal government superior to the states. The South, like the Anti-Federalists, believed in state power over federal. The South attempted to leave the Union. This resulted in the American Civil War. Four bloody years later the South lay in ruins and the North was victorious. Slavery and the more than seventy year conflict between the states and the federal government were over. The federal government was superior to the states. The power of the Supreme Court to review both federal and state laws remained intact.

Taney's decision in the *Dred Scott* case was, in effect, overturned—not by the Supreme Court or an act of Congress, but by changing the Constitution itself. The Supreme Court is the final word on what the Constitution means, but the Constitution can be changed or amended. On December 18, 1865, the nation ratified the Thirteenth Amendment to the Constitution, officially ending slavery in the United States.

10

Judicial Review in the Early Twentieth Century

Today *Marbury* v. *Madison* is seen as the single most important decision in Supreme Court history—not because of what happened in 1803 or the rest of the nineteenth century, but because of what has happened since then. During the nineteenth century, the Supreme Court rarely used judicial review to strike down laws, especially federal laws. During this period, the Court rarely cited *Marbury* v. *Madison.* As the twentieth century approached, judicial power increased, and with it, the legacy of *Marbury* v. *Madison* was born.

From the 1890s to the 1930s the United States saw a great increase in immigration and industrialization. Laws were passed that attempted to regulate these increases. In the early twentieth century any attempt by lawmakers to regulate industry was seen as extreme. The nation was changing rapidly. The Constitution was not.

The Supreme Court case of *Lochner* v. *New York* was the beginning of thirty years of judicial review the likes of which had never been seen before. Both the states and the federal government were trying to curb the abuses of big business. The Supreme Court would review, and often strike down, economic and social laws meant to protect the people.

In the *Lochner* case, the Supreme Court reviewed a New York law setting maximum hours for bakers to work. It was 1905 and bakers, along with other workers, were working dangerously long hours. This situation was presenting a health risk that New York was attempting to combat. The Supreme Court struck down the New York law, claiming it violated the Contract Clause of the Constitution. The Contract Clause states that no state shall pass a "law impairing the obligation of contracts."[1] In its majority opinion the Supreme Court wrote that "freedom of master and employee to contract with each other in relation to their employment. . .cannot be prohibited or interfered with, without violating the federal Constitution."[2] By virtue of judicial review the Supreme Court was tying the hands of government in its attempt to combat abuses to the working class.

Did the drafters of the Constitution really intend for the Contract Clause to prohibit government from in any way regulating business? Or is it possible that the Supreme Court was making a political decision?

In *Marbury* v. *Madison,* Marshall recognized that the power of judicial review was a limited power. He warned that the Supreme Court does not, nor should it, have the power to review political questions. That is, the Court does not have the power to inquire as to how politicians "perform duties in which they have a discretion."[3]

In his dissenting opinion in *Lochner,* Justice John Marshall Harlan wrote, "Under our system of government . . . the courts are not concerned with the wisdom or policy of legislation."[4] Harlan suggested, as have many legal historians, that the decision in *Lochner* was based not on the freedom of contract but rather on a political issue. In its opinion the Court claims, "This is not a question of substituting the judgment of the Court for that of the legislature."[5] But in the same opinion the Court writes, "We do not believe in the soundness of the views which uphold this law."[6] Could it be that the Supreme Court just did not agree with the law and framed the opinion to find a Constitutional violation?

Lochner was just the beginning of a thirty-year period in which the Supreme Court would often substitute its judgment for that of Congress and state lawmakers. Between 1900 and 1937, the Court would strike down over one hundred fifty state laws. Even the federal government was not immune. During the 1920s the Court struck down twenty laws passed by Congress. This is more than in the entire previous half-century.[7] Because most of these laws dealt with social and economic issues, the period between the 1890s and 1930s is often called "the *Lochner* era."

Thomas Jefferson's battle with the Supreme Court was the first of many between a president and the judiciary. It is Congress that makes the law, but the president, executes the law, makes policy, and often proposes laws for the Congress to vote on. It is frustrating for a president to succeed in convincing Congress to pass a law only to have it struck down by the Supreme Court. This presidential frustration has ignited some bitter clashes between the executive and judicial branches.

In 1932 Franklin D. Roosevelt was elected president. The Great Depression had already started and the United States was in economic turmoil. Across the country there was massive unemployment. People lost their life savings in the stock market and declines in farm income were common. There were widespread bank and business failures, and people were losing their farms and homes in mortgage foreclosures. Americans wanted the government to do something. Roosevelt was elected because he promised he would.

Before the Depression, the United States, like most western governments, had done little regarding the economy. The prevailing view was to let the economy run itself. The Constitution was vague as to the power that Congress had in relationship to the economy. It gave Congress the power to tax and spend; "to pay the Debts and provide for the . . . general Welfare of the United States"; and "[t]o regulate Commerce with foreign Nations, and among the several states. . . ."[8] These powers left a great deal of room for interpretation. If interpreted narrowly, congressional power to regulate the economy would be very limited. If interpreted broadly, the power would be great.

Roosevelt came through on his promise. In a short time he passed through Congress the most progressive economic laws in history. The package was called the "New Deal." The New Deal was a series of acts creating governmental agencies meant to employ the people, build highways and dams, improve agricultural output, and regulate the economy.

Roosevelt cleared the first hurdle, Congress. He knew, however, that in a short time the Supreme Court would review the New Deal.

Like Thomas Jefferson, Roosevelt found himself a president with a rival party dominating the Supreme Court. Roosevelt was a Democrat. He was only the third democrat elected to the presidency since the Civil War. The Supreme Court was dominated by Justices appointed by past Republican presidents. While campaigning in 1932, Roosevelt realized that the Republicans had "complete control of all branches of the Federal Government . . . the Supreme Court as well."[9]

The National Industrial Recovery Act was passed in 1933. It was the New Deal's first major act, meant to give the people economic relief. It prescribed codes of fair competition among businesses and established a minimum wage and maximum work hours. In 1935, the Supreme Court reviewed the act in the case of *Schechter Poultry Corp.* v. *United States.* The Supreme Court took a narrow interpretation of the congressional power to regulate businesses and the economy. The Court struck down the law, claiming that Congress went beyond the powers granted to it by the Commerce Clause of the Constitution.

The Supreme Court went on to strike down numerous other New Deal laws. Between 1934 and 1936 the Court invalidated thirteen federal laws as well as many state laws meant to combat the Depression. The Court reasoned that Congress was going beyond the powers granted to it by the Constitution. It seemed that the Court would not budge from this interpretation. Every New Deal law was in jeopardy of being invalidated.

Roosevelt accepted judicial review, yet he believed that the Court was abusing the power. He concluded that "[John] Marshall's conception of our Constitution as a flexible instrument—adequate for all times, and, therefore, able to adjust itself as new needs of new generations arose—had been repudiated."[10] This meant that Marshall's view of a Constitution that would change with the times had been abandoned.

The country needed economic reform, and Roosevelt thought the New Deal laws were the answer. But, with the Supreme Court as it stood, the New Deal was doomed. What could he or any other president do in these circumstances? He did not have the constitutional authority to fire the Justices. Nor did he have a realistic chance to impeach them. Roosevelt considered attempting to amend the Constitution. The amendment would limit the power of the Supreme Court to invalidate acts of Congress. This would, in effect, eliminate the power of judicial review. Such an amendment would require the overwhelming support of both Congress and the people. Although he was a popular and powerful president, Roosevelt knew he would not have the support needed for such an amendment.

Roosevelt decide to propose that Congress give him the power to appoint more Justices. The Constitution does not specify exactly how many Justices the Supreme Court can have. The number has been as few as five and as many as ten. From 1869 until today, Congress has provided for nine Justices to serve on the Supreme Court. If Roosevelt could pack the Court with additional Justices who were sympathetic to the New Deal, then a majority of the Court could uphold the programs. Roosevelt proclaimed: "[W]e must take action to save the Constitution from the Court and the Court from itself."[11] The proposal would become known as the court packing plan.

Like Jefferson before him, Roosevelt would fail to convince Congress and the people to adopt his proposal. While the majority of Congress and the people did not like the Court's decisions, they would not allow the president to interfere with its independence.

Throughout the 1930s the Supreme Court found many laws initiated by Franklin Roosevelt unconstitutional. To put a stop to this, Roosevelt attempted to add enough Justices to the Supreme Court to outvote the judges who were voting against his policies. This cartoon makes fun of his idea to add more Justices to the Court.

The Court-packing plan failed. Yet it served as a wake up call to the stubborn Supreme Court. In the case of *West Coast Hotel* v. *Parrish,* the Court, in a five to four decision, upheld a Washington minimum-wage law. This was a complete turn around from its decision striking down a similar law in *Schechter Poultry Corp.* v. *United States.* The Court went on to uphold other New Deal laws that it would surely have struck down before the court-packing plan. In the end, the Supreme Court broadened its interpretation of Congress's constitutional powers. In this way Congress's power to regulate the economy was expanded. The New Deal survived, and the United States eventually exited the Depression.

11

Modern Judicial Review

Marbury v. *Madison* is more important today than it ever was in the nineteenth century. In the twenty-five years from 1958 to 1983, there were eighty-nine separate citations of the decision in Supreme Court opinions. This almost equals the total of the previous one hundred and fifty-four years. The question in modern Supreme Court history is not whether the Court has the power of judicial review, but how often it will be used.

This question can be answered by seeing who is in control of the Supreme Court. Justices have one of two basic philosophies when it comes to judicial review. There are the traditionalists who interpret the constitution narrowly. These individuals rule according to the exact meaning of the words of the Constitution. They, like Marshall, use a great deal of judicial restraint. That is, they defer to Congress on social and economic issues. They base their decisions on what the Founding Fathers intended the Constitution to mean. Believing in precedents, following past court decisions, they rarely reverse Supreme Court decisions.

The other philosophy is the activist view. The activists take a very broad approach to constitutional interpretation. They go beyond the plain meaning of the words of the Constitution and look at what these words may imply. They believe that Constitutional interpretation should change with the times. This philosophy allows the Court to play a large role in bringing about political, social, and economic change.

In the past fifty years we have seen activists and traditionalists on the Supreme Court. We have also seen many Justices somewhere in between the two. The Court sometimes takes on the philosophy of its Chief Justice. This is because the president who appoints the Chief Justice is likely to have appointed numerous other Justices of the same philosophy. We have seen the Supreme Court sway from the liberal-thinking activists of the 1950s, 1960s, and 1970s to the more conservative-minded traditionalists of the 1980s and 1990s. In this chapter we will explore how Marshall's tool of judicial review has been used from 1953 to today.

In 1953 President Eisenhower, a Republican, appointed Earl Warren as Chief Justice of the Supreme Court. Earl Warren was a very successful Republican politician. He had served as Attorney General for the state of California. He also served three terms as its governor. In 1948, he was the unsuccessful Republican candidate for vice-president. Most expected Warren to be a fairly traditionalist Chief Justice, but this was not to be. Warren was surrounded by activist Justices appointed by the previous two Democratic presidents. Instead of his being in conflict with their philosophies, it turned out that he shared them. The Warren Court was the most activist Supreme Court in history.

In 1954 the Warren Court used the activist philosophy to reverse an unjust ruling that had affected the nation since 1898. The issue was school segregation. In many parts of the country, school systems had separate schools for black and white students. Civil rights activists argued that segregation violated the Equal Protection Clause of the Fourteenth Amendment. This amendment, ratified just after the Civil War, prohibits the states from making any law that would "deny to any person within its jurisdiction the equal protection of the laws." Thus the states could not deny one person a benefit given to another person under a law.

At first glance, it appears that these activists had a

good argument. The only problem was that the same argument had been made to the Supreme Court in 1898 in the case of *Plessy* v. *Ferguson.* The Court found that segregation was not unconstitutional so long as railroad cars had equal facilities for blacks and whites. This was called the doctrine of separate but equal.

Fifty-six years later in 1954, the Supreme Court tackled the issue of school segregation. The case was *Brown* v. *Board of Education.* A Kansas law permitted cities with more than fifteen thousand residents to operate segregated schools. The law also said that if these cities decided to segregate, they must have substantially equal facilities. In this way, the law was consistent with the separate but equal doctrine of *Plessy* v. *Ferguson.*

To rule in favor of the civil rights leaders, the Supreme Court would have to reverse its own ruling. It is very important that the Supreme Court follow precedent. This is called the doctrine of *stare decisis.* It means the Court should rule the same way on a given issue as in previous decisions, even if the Justices' views were now different. It is vital that the Supreme Court is consistent in its rulings so that the rest of us know what the law is. If the Court were to rule differently from year to year then lawmakers would not know if the laws they were writing would withstand judicial review. It is

Earl Warren was appointed Chief Justice of the Supreme Court in 1953. Under Warren, legalized segregation was found unconstitutional when the *Plessy* v. *Ferguson* decision of 1898 was reversed by the ruling in *Brown* v. *Board of Education.*

extremely rare that a Supreme Court reverses one of its prior decisions. But this is exactly what the Warren Court did.

In *Brown,* the Court noted that the segregated public schools were equal in size, buildings, curricula, and qualification of teachers. It, however, went further and looked at "the effect of segregation itself on public education."[1] It found that segregation was usually interpreted by students as suggesting inferiority of African-American students. This, of course, is a barrier in a child's motivation to learn. The Court found that "separate educational facilities are inherently unequal."[2] The Kansas law was struck down as violating the Fourteenth Amendment, and *Plessy* v. *Ferguson* was reversed.

Many southern states were outraged at the Court's decision. Arkansas's governor and lawmakers claimed they were not bound by the *Brown* decision and refused to desegregate. In *Cooper* v. *Aaron* (1958) the Supreme Court reaffirmed the *Brown* decision. All nine justices signed the opinion rejecting Arkansas's argument that it was not bound by the Court's decision. The Court cited *Marbury* v. *Madison* in declaring its supremacy over the states and added:

> This decision declared the basic principle that the federal judiciary is supreme in the exposition of the law of the Constitution. [It] follows that the interpretation of the Fourteenth Amendment enunciated by this Court

> in the Brown case is the Supreme Law of the land, and Article VI of the Constitution makes it of binding effect on the states.[3]

Another characteristic of an activist court is the use of implied rights. An implied right, as opposed to an enumerated right, is not specifically granted by the Constitution, but instead is read into it by the courts. An enumerated right is a right specifically granted by the Constitution. The First Amendment's freedom of speech is an example of an enumerated right.

In the case of *Griswold* v. *Connecticut,* the Warren Court used an implied right to strike down a Connecticut law in 1965. The law made it a crime to use or provide another person with information about contraceptives. The Supreme Court claimed this violated the Constitutional right to privacy. Nowhere in the Constitution does it specifically grant people the right to privacy. No Court before the Warren Court ever recognized the right of privacy. The Court reasoned that the enumerated rights such as the First Amendment's freedom of association, the Fifth Amendment's protection against self-incrimination, and the Fourth Amendment's protection against unreasonable search and seizures "create zones of privacy."[4] As such, there is an implied constitutional right to privacy.

In his dissenting opinion, Justice Potter Stewart had

the same thoughts that most traditionalists did about the *Griswold* decision. He admitted that the Connecticut law was a "silly law."[5] He also said, however, that the Court should not "substitute their social and economic beliefs for the judgment of legislative bodies, who are elected to pass laws."[6]

A great many Americans thought that the Supreme Court was abusing the power of judicial review and infringing on the authority of lawmakers. In 1969 one such American had a chance to change this. Richard Nixon, a Republican, was president when Earl Warren retired as Chief Justice. Nixon wanted a conservative Supreme Court. Warren E. Burger was a United States Court of Appeals Judge in the District of Columbia circuit. He was thought to be a conservative judge who would undo the activism of the Warren Court. In 1969, he was appointed by Nixon as Chief Justice. Like Eisenhower, Nixon was disappointed.

In its first ten years, the Burger Court changed little from the Warren Court. The Court continued to use judicial review to bring about political, social, and economic change. The 1973 case of *Roe* v. *Wade* gave the Court the opportunity, once again, to use the implied right of privacy to strike down a law. This was a Texas law that prohibited abortions, except when it was necessary to save the life of the pregnant woman. The Court wrote:

> This right to privacy, whether it be found in the Fourteenth Amendment's concept of personal liberty [as] we feel it does, [or] in the Ninth Amendment's reservation of rights to the people, is broad enough to encompass a woman's decision whether or not to terminate her pregnancy.[7]

Although the Court ruled that abortion was a right covered under the Constitution, it was not an absolute right. States could still regulate and even prohibit abortions late in the pregnancy.

The Burger Court also used judicial review to change the criminal justice system. In a series of cases in 1972, the Burger Court struck down all then-existing state death penalty laws. The immediate effect of these rulings was that no crime could be punished by execution. Some of the Burger Court Justices felt that the death penalty violated the Eighth Amendment's prohibition against cruel and unusual punishment. The Supreme Court, however, had never before ruled that the death penalty violated the Eighth Amendment. It is also clear that the Founding Fathers did not intend the Eighth Amendment to prohibit the death penalty. Capital punishment, the death penalty, existed before, during, and after the Eighth Amendment was ratified. The true intent of the Eighth Amendment was to

Chief Justice Warren Burger is shown here. Like the Warren Court, the Burger Court used judicial review to bring about political, social, and economic change.

prohibit torture or other punishment that did not fit the crime. The activist philosophy, however, does not necessarily take into account what the Founding Fathers intended two hundred years ago. The activists believe we must consider societal changes in our culture and politics. At least two members of the Burger Court believed that today's standards of decency had evolved into making the death penalty unconstitutional.

Other Burger Court Justices believed that the death penalty procedures were unfair. They believed that the manner in which one was prosecuted under then existing death penalty laws was arbitrary. Thus, these laws violated the Eighth Amendment. They lacked guidelines for sentencing and permitted the indiscriminate imposition of the death penalty. There was also evidence of race being a factor in who was and who was not subject to the death penalty. A black man was more likely than a white man to be executed for the same crime.

In these decisions the Supreme Court challenged Congress and the state lawmakers to rework the death-penalty laws. In this way, a judge and jury could use discretion in sentencing. At the same time, they could reduce the likelihood of abusing discretion by setting sentencing guidelines. In 1976, the states of Georgia, Texas, and Florida enacted death-penalty laws that were reviewed by the Supreme Court. These laws provided a two-stage procedure. The first stage was the guilt-innocent phase. Here the judge and jury trying the case decided if the person on trial actually committed the crime. If the person was found guilty, he or she went on to the second phase. The second phase was the punishment phase, in which those trying the case decided between death and a prison sentence. In the second phase those trying the case hear factors such as the person's past record and the circumstances surrounding the crime to help reach a decision. These laws survived the judicial review of the Burger Court in *Gregg* v. *Georgia* in 1976.

Soon other states adopted death-penalty laws similar to those of Georgia, Texas, and Florida. These, too, survived judicial review. A minority of Justices felt that the death penalty was cruel and unusual in any form. The majority, however, felt that the safeguards of these new laws conformed to constitutional restrictions.

The most conservative Justice on the Burger Court was William H. Rehnquist. During the Burger Court years he often found himself the lone dissenter on Court decisions. Rehnquist did not agree with the activist philosophy of the other Justices. He was a traditionalist. He saw the Court's function as enforcing explicit guarantees such as the ones spelled out in the

Bill of Rights. He did not believe in the implied rights that the Court read into the Constitution. Rehnquist felt it was important to enforce the explicit guarantees of the Constitution. At the same time, there should be respect for the decisions of the political branches of government. In this way, the Court would uphold the integrity of the separation of powers.

William Rehnquist was appointed to the Supreme Court in 1972 by Richard Nixon. In 1986, Ronald Reagan appointed Rehnquist Chief Justice when Warren Burger retired. President Reagan, a conservative Republican, was able to surround Rehnquist with other conservative Justices whenever there was a vacancy in the Supreme Court. Soon the Court took on the philosophy of Rehnquist. From 1986 until today, the Supreme Court has often used judicial discretion by upholding laws.

The Rehnquist Court has consistently deferred to the judgment of the lawmakers. It has upheld laws that may have been struck down by the Warren and Burger Courts. The 1989 case of *Webster* v. *Reproductive Health Services* dealt with a Missouri law that prohibited abortions in any public hospital. It also prohibited any public funds from being used to finance abortions. The Court upheld the law, but surprised some by not completely overruling *Roe* v. *Wade*. Although there was a right to have an abortion, states did not have to finance them. The Court continued to uphold laws that placed restrictions on abortions, but stopped short of outlawing them. Justice Sandra Day O'Connor wrote: "The central holding of *Roe* v. *Wade* must be reaffirmed. . . . Some of us as individuals find abortion offensive to our most basic principles of morality, but that cannot control our decision."[8]

All Supreme Court Justices have had to deal with

President Ronald Reagan appointed William Rehnquist (shown here) as Chief Justice once Warren Burger retired. The Rehnquist Court was more conservative than both the Burger and Warren Courts.

laws about which they have strong feelings. The Justices, however, particularly those that follow the traditionalist philosophy, must ignore those feelings and decide only if the law violates the Constitution. In the case of *U.S.* v. *Eichman* (1990), the Court had to decide on the constitutionality of the Flag Protection Act. This was a federal law making it a crime to knowingly mutilate, deface, or burn the American flag. The Court, using judicial review, struck down the law as violating the First Amendment's protection of freedom of speech and expression. Flag burning is a form of symbolic speech and is therefore protected under the First Amendment.

William Jefferson Clinton, a more liberal democrat, was elected president of the United States in 1992. He was reelected in 1996. Clinton had the opportunity to change the philosophy of the Supreme Court. In 1993 he appointed Ruth Bader Ginsburg to the Court. As a judge on the court of appeals for the District of Columbia, Ginsburg has a national reputation for fighting for women's rights. In 1994 Clinton appointed Stephen G. Breyer to the Court. Breyer was on the circuit court of appeals in Boston and has shown an interest in protecting individual and civil rights. The Court may yet swing back from traditionalist to activist.

Questions for Discussion

For a federal law to pass, it must obtain a majority in both the House of Representatives and the Senate. It must also survive the veto power of the president. Congress, the House of Representatives and the Senate, are elected by the people of their individual states to represent their interests. So when a law is passed, it is the people who are making the law. The people also elect the president. The president has veto power. When a law is passed by Congress, the president has the power to reject it and send it back to Congress. Congress must then pass the law by a two-thirds majority, or the law fails. A law is a difficult thing to create and it is created only if the majority of elected officials agree.

Should we have judicial review?

Judicial review allows five Justices who are never elected by the people to strike down a law passed by the people. There are nine Supreme Court Justices. It takes five to create a majority. If five believe a law is in violation of the Constitution, they can strike it down.

Does this seem undemocratic?

Many people argue that judicial review is undemocratic and should be ended. Supreme Court Justices are not elected and serve life terms. The only way they leave the Court is by retirement, impeachment, or death. The Court, therefore, does not have to answer to the people. Laws that are extremely popular with the people can be, and have been, struck down by the Court. The Flag Protection Act struck down by the Court in *U.S.* v. *Eichman* was an extremely popular law. The year before the case, a *Newsweek* poll showed 71 percent of the people supported a constitutional amendment similar to the Act.[1] Yet, by a five to four vote, the Supreme Court struck down the law.

Unlike the political branches of the government, the Supreme Court does not have to answer directly to the people. This is the way the Constitution intended it. The Supreme Court does not answer political questions. It answers legal questions. It is not supposed to determine if a law is wise or just, but rather if it is legal. Since the Justices do not have to worry about losing their jobs, they can rule on law without fear. Thus the Court feels free to strike down even popular laws that violate the Constitution. How do you feel about this? Support your answer.

What if the Supreme Court strikes down a law that is important to the country?

The Supreme Court is the final word on what the Constitution means. But the people have the final word on what form the Constitution takes. The people have the power to add to, take away from, or change the Constitution. This is done by amending the Constitution. Amendments to the Constitution require a great deal of support and are therefore very rare. In fact, there have only been twenty-seven amendments to our Constitution in its history. The last time was 1992, when members of Congress were prevented from passing immediate salary increases for themselves.

Do you feel the system of amending the Constitution is a fair one? Support your answer.

The Civil War was the most devastating war in United States history. The war was fought for many reasons, but the most important was over the issue of slavery. Even after the war the federal government could not pass a law prohibiting slavery throughout the country. Why? Because of the Supreme Court's decision in *Dred*

Scott v. *Sandford* (1856). That case struck down the Missouri Compromise and ruled that the federal government could not outlaw slavery in the territories. The Civil War, which ended in 1865, did not change that fact. The only thing that could change that was a Constitutional amendment. In 1865 the Thirteenth Amendment to the Constitution ended slavery throughout the country. Thus, an important law that is struck down by the Supreme Court can be made constitutional by amending the Constitution.

You Be the Judge

Assume that the following laws are passed by the federal government. You are a Supreme Court Justice who must decide if these laws violate the Constitution. The relevant sections of the Constitution are provided for reference. Decide if you are going to use judicial review to strike down the law or judicial restraint and let the law survive. Also, determine which philosophy you hold: Are you a traditionalist or an activist? If you are working with others, hold a vote. The majority decides if the law survives or is struck down.

Law I: NO RESIDENTIAL HOUSEHOLD SHALL POSSESS AT ANY ONE TIME MORE THAN THREE FIREARMS.

Second Amendment: A well-regulated militia, being necessary to the security of a free state, the right of the people to keep and bear arms, shall not be infringed.

First, see if you want to use the traditionalist philosophy to decide if Law I violates the Second

Amendment. Remember, you are not to decide on the wisdom of the law, but rather whether or not it violates the Constitution.

Examine the traditional approach to Constitutional interpretation. A traditionalist interprets the Constitution narrowly. The traditionalist would use the exact meaning of the words. The word "shall" as opposed the word "may" indicates a requirement that the government not infringe on the people's rights to bear arms. The words "keep or bear" would clearly fall under law I's word "possess." So, looking at the exact meaning, the government cannot infringe on the people's right to possess firearms. We must now decide what the word "infringe," as used in the Second Amendment means. The dictionary defines infringe as "to break off, break, impair, violate."[1] Law I does not prohibit one from possessing firearms. It does, however, limit the number one may possess. As a traditionalist you may find that any impairment or violation, however slight, is an "infringement."

The traditionalists also look to what the Founding Fathers intended. The Second Amendment actually tells us what they meant. It indicates that the right is important because "[a] well-regulated militia, [is] necessary to the security of a free state." The Revolutionary War was fought largely by citizen soldiers (militia) as opposed to a regular army. These people kept their own weapons in their homes. To deter foreign invaders and the people in government from trying to establish a military dictatorship, the Founding Fathers wanted to guarantee the people's right to possess firearms. They wanted the people to be able to rise up if necessary and fight tyranny. In terms of the intent of the Founding Fathers, does Law I violate the purpose of the Second Amendment?

Now examine the activist approach to Constitutional interpretation. Activists interpret very broadly. They go beyond the exact meaning of the words to interpret what they Founding Fathers may have meant and how it applies to society today. You may have to look more at the wisdom of the law and then justify your decision under the Constitution.

As an activist, you must decide if the law brings about a desirable change and if the Constitution is interpreted to support such a change. In the recent past, violent crime has increased, and so has the amount of firearms used in these crimes. The law, by limiting the number of firearms a person can have, will limit the number of firearms produced. This may limit the number of firearms used in crime. It would also limit the number of firearms that can be stolen from a single home and then sold on the streets.

If you feel this law has a desirable effect, you might

interpret the Second Amendment broadly enough not to find a violation. Remember, it is the activist's view that the Constitution should change with the times. You may interpret the Second Amendment's word "infringed" to mean prohibit. Law I does not prohibit one from possessing a firearm, it only limits the number a household may possess. As such, you might uphold Law I as constitutional.

You must now decide if you are going to strike down the law as unconstitutional. If you are with others, vote on your decision. Be prepared to support your decision. You may choose to write an opinion to explain your decision. If you are in the minority, you may write a dissenting opinion. When you are finished, continue this process with the next law.

Law II: IT SHALL BE A CRIME PUNISHABLE BY UP TO FIVE YEARS IN PRISON FOR ANYONE TO SUPPORT THE OVERTHROW OF THE GOVERNMENT BY FORCE OR VIOLENCE.

The First Amendment: Congress shall make no law respecting an establishment of religion, or prohibiting the free exercise thereof; or abridging the freedom of speech or of the press; or the right of the people peaceably to assemble, and to petition the government for a redress of grievances.

Does Law II violate the First Amendment? This time, let's do some legal research to assist us in deciding. A very important tool used by both traditionalists and activists is case law. Case law is not law passed by lawmakers, but rather decisions made by the courts. When a court makes a decision interpreting a law or the Constitution, that interpretation becomes case law. All courts lower than the court making the decision must follow that case law. The Supreme Court is the highest court in the land, so when it makes case law all other courts must follow it. The Supreme Court follows its own case law whenever possible. This is called precedent. So when deciding an issue, the Supreme Court will look to its past decisions and examine them.

Let's examine some old Supreme Court cases dealing with the First Amendment and laws that restrict support for the overthrow of government.

The first case to examine is *Schenck* v. *United States* (1919). In this case, the Supreme Court upheld the Espionage Act of 1917. This act was passed as the United States entered World War I. The act made it a crime to support resistance to the war effort. Schenck was a communist who urged prospective draftees not to allow themselves to be drafted. He was convicted under the Espionage Act and appealed the case to the Supreme Court. Schenck claimed that the act violated the First Amendment's right to free speech and assembly.

The Supreme Court came up with a test to see if a law violates freedom of speech and assembly.

> The question in every case is whether the words used are used in such circumstances and are of such a nature as to create a clear and present danger that they will bring about the substantive evils that Congress has a right to prevent.[2]

The Supreme Court upheld the Espionage Act of 1917. This, however, does not mean that you must uphold Law II. You must look at all the circumstances surrounding a prior case. One important factor in the *Schenck* case is the time it took place. The nation had entered World War I by the time the act was in effect. During a time of peace, the same Supreme Court may have found that the Espionage Act did not pass the "clear and present danger test." Thus, during a time of peace, the Espionage Act may violate the First Amendment.

The *Schenck* case is of great help to us because it gives us a test to apply to Law II. Before you apply the "clear and present danger" test, let's look to see if there is a more recent case dealing with the same issue. It would be helpful to find a case that has applied the test to a law similar to Law II.

In the *Schenck* case the Supreme Court upheld the Espionage Act, but it is important to remember the circumstances and historical events that took place at that time. Use the "clear and present danger" test to decide if Law II is in violation of the First Amendment. Law II is meant to prevent the violent overthrow of the government. This is an "evil that Congress has a right to prevent." But does Law II prohibit only those words used that create a "clear and present danger" or does it go too far and prohibit words that are protected under the First Amendment? If we are in a time of peace, with little risk of an overthrow of the government, is Law II necessary to prevent a "clear and present danger?"

In *Brandenburg* the Supreme Court struck down the Ohio Criminal Syndicalism Act as violating the First Amendment. At the time of the *Brandenburg* case, there was little risk of a government overthrow.[3] That act was similar but not the same as Law II. Both, however, do punish for the support of force or violence. Law II is not specific as to what words are illegal. The Supreme Court in *Brandenburg* criticized the act's broad and nonspecific wording.[4] It found that mere support was not enough to overcome the First Amendment protections. Only if the law prohibits words that incite "imminent" or immediate "lawless action" will the law be found constitutional.

Use the same process used in deciding Law I's constitutionality to make your decision. Does Law II violate the First Amendment?

Chapter Notes

Chapter 1

No notes.

Chapter 2

1. United States Constitution, Article VI.

2. United States Constitution, Amendment X.

3. Alien and Sedition Acts.

4. M.J. Smith, *Freedom's Fetters* (Ithaca, N.Y.: Cornell University Press, 1956), pp. 94–95.

5. T.I. Emerson, D. Harber, and N. Doresen, *Political and Civil Rights in the United States* (New York: Random House, 1967), p. 38.

Chapter 3

1. W. Seagle, *Men of Law* (New York: The Macmillan Company, 1948), p. 279.

2. Ibid., p. 282.

3. Ibid.

4. Robert F. Cushman, *Leading Constitutional Decisions,* 18th ed., (Englewood Cliffs, N.J.: Prentice Hall Publishers, Inc., 1992), p. 1.

Chapter 4

1. United States Constitution, Article III.

2. Don Reilly, Norman Murphy, and Chuck Timus, *The Supreme Court: Its Beginnings and its Justices 1790–1991* (Washington, D.C.: Commission on the Bicentennial of the United States Constitution, 1992), p. 12.

Chapter 5

1. *Marbury* v. *Madison,* 5 U.S. 137 (1 Cranch), (1803).
2. Ibid.
3. Ibid.
4. United States Constitution, Article III, section 2.
5. *Marbury* v. *Madison,* 5 U.S. 137 (1 Cranch), (1803).
6. Ibid.
7. Ibid.
8. Ibid.
9. Ibid.

Chapter 6

1. J.C. Miller, *Crisis in Freedom: the Alien and Sedition Acts* (Boston: Little Brown 1952), p. 113.

Chapter 7

1. Robert J. Wagman, *The Supreme Court: A Citizen's Guide* (New York: Pharos Books, 1993), p. 48.
2. Alexander Hamilton, John Jay, and James Madison, *The Federalist Papers* (Cutchogue, New York: Buccaneer Books, 1992), p. 395.
3. Ibid.

Chapter 8

1. *McCulloch* v. *Maryland,* 17 U.S. (Wheat) 316 (1819).
2. The United States Constitution, Article 1, section 8.
3. *McCulloch* v. *Maryland,* 17 U.S. (Wheat) 316 (1819).
4. Ibid.
5. *Fletcher* v. *Peck,* 10 U.S. 6 (Cranch) 87 (1810).

Chapter 9

No notes.

Chapter 10

1. The United States Constitution, Article I, section 10.
2. *Lochner* v. *New York,* 198 U.S. 45 (1905).

3. Ibid.

4. Ibid.

5. Ibid.

6. Ibid.

7. Elder Witt, *The Supreme Court A to Z* (Washington, D.C.: Congressional Quarterly Books, 1994).

8. The United States Constitution, Article I, section 8.

9. Leonard W. Levy, ed., *Encyclopedia of the American Constitution* (New York: Macmillan Publishing Company, 1986) p. 1605.

10. Ibid., p. 1606.

11. Ibid.

Chapter 11

1. *Brown* v. *Board of Education,* 347 U.S. 483 (1954).

2. Ibid.

3. *Cooper* v. *Aaron,* 358 U.S. 1 (1958).

4. *Griswold* v. *Connecticut,* 381 U.S. 479 (1965).

5. Ibid.

6. Ibid.

7. *Roe* v. *Wade,* 410 U.S. 113 (1973).

8. *Planned Parenthood of Southern Pennsylvania* v. *Casey,* 505 U.S. 833 (1992).

Questions for Discussion

1. Tamar Jacoby, "A Fight for Old Glory," *Newsweek,* July 3, 1989, p. 18.

You be the Judge

1. *Webster's New World Dictionary,* second college edition, Springfield, Mass.:, 1993, p. 600.

2. *Schenck* v. *United States,* 249 U.S. 47 (1919).

3. *Brandenburg* v. *Ohio,* 395 U.S. 444 (1969).

4. Ibid.

Glossary

acquittal—To be found not guilty of a crime.

activist—A philosophical interpretation of the Constitution in which the interpreter takes into consideration modern social and political views.

amendment—An addition or change to the Constitution.

Anti-Federalists—Members of an early American political party who desired a weak federal government in favor of power to the individual states.

appeal—A proceeding in which a higher court reviews a lower court decision.

Articles of Confederation—The first formal document forming a government after the American Revolution. This document was abandoned in favor of the more unifying Constitution of the United States of America.

certiorari—A writ or court order to review a lower court decision.

circuit courts—Federal courts that would review decisions of the district courts and could only be reviewed by the Supreme Court.

concurring opinion—An opinion that a Justice may write that agrees with the majority of the court but for different reasons.

Continental Congress—A body of government made up of representatives of the individual colonies at the time of the American Revolution.

dissenting opinion—An opinion a Justice may write that disagrees with the majority opinion.

district courts—Federal courts that actually hear evidence (trial courts). Decisions by these courts can be reviewed by circuit courts.

enumerated powers—Those powers specifically granted to government by the Constitution.

Federalists—Members of an early American political party who favored a strong federal government with limited state power.

"Federalist Papers"—A series of articles written to explain the proposed Constitution. They were specifically meant to convince the people of New York to ratify the Constitution.

impeach—To remove a public official from office for misconduct.

implied powers—Those powers not specifically granted to government by the Constitution but that are necessary and proper for government to perform its enumerated powers.

majority opinion—A court's decision. It is binding on all parties as well as all inferior courts.

original jurisdiction—The place or court where a legal action, prosecution, or law suit must originate.

president-elect—The individual who has been elected president but who has not yet assumed the duties of office.

precedent—A court ruling that may serve as authority for a subsequent similar rulings in similar circumstances.

stare decisis—A policy of following rules laid down in previous judicial decisions.

traditionalists—Those who look at the plain meaning and original intention of the writers of the Constitution.

Further Reading

Burger, Warren E. *It is So Ordered: A Constitution Unfolds.* New York: William Morrow and Company Inc., 1995.

Eastlan, Terry. *Benchmarks: Great Constitutional Controversies in the Supreme Court.* Washington, D. C.: Ethics and Public Policy Center, 1995.

Feinberg, Barbara Silberdick. *John Marshall: The Great Chief Justice.* Springfield, N.J.: Enslow Publishers, Inc., 1995.

Green, Carl and William R. Sanford. *American Government: The Judiciary.* Vero Beach, Fla.: Rourke Publishing Company, 1990

Hauptly, Denis J. *A Convention of Delegates.* New York: Antheneun, 1978.

Jenkins, George H. *American Government: The Constitution.* Vero Beach, Fla.: Rouke Publishing Company, 1990.

Kluge, Dave. *The Peoples Guide to The United Sates Constitution.* New York: Carol Publishing Group, 1994.

Ley, Leonard W. *Seasoned Judgments: The American Constitution, Rights, and History.* New Brunswick, N.J.: Transaction Publishers, 1995.

Mabie, Margot G. J. *The Constitution: Reflection of a Changing Nation.* New York: Henry Holt and Company, 1987.

Ritchie, Donald A. *Know Your Government: The U. S. Constitution.* New York: Chelsea House Publishers, 1989.

Index